The Essentials of An Effective Sales Strategy

by Felix Kaufman

Table of Contents

Forces in the Marketing Environment.................... 6
   Demographic and Cultural Understanding.............. 6
   Microeconomic Understanding of The Economy... 7
   Technological Changes 7
   Competing with Others 7

Perfecting the Sales Pitch.. 8
   The 7 Ps of Marketing... 8
      Product.. 8
      Price.. 9
      Promotion... 9
      Product Placement 9
      People 10
      Physical Evidence 11

Persuasive Storytelling... 12
   Storytelling Examples... 12

Lead Optimization.. 14
   Challenges with Lead Generation.......................... 14
      Nurturing Approach.. 14
      Data Enrichment.. 15
      Sales Qualified Lead (SQL)............................... 15
   Lead Optimization Examples................................ 15

Post-Sale Follow Up 17
   Frequency of Follow-ups....................................... 17

Smart Trials and Onboarding Customers.............. 19
   Length of The Trial... 19

    Trial Offer Example...................................19
  Onboarding Customers..21
    Onboarding Example...............................21
Time Marketing..22
  Questions for Time Marketers...............................22
PAS System...24
  Problem..24
  Agitate..25
  Solution 25
  PAS Example...25
Finding Specific Referrals..27
  Referral Marketing Examples.................................28
Viral Marketing...29
  Viral Marketing Platforms......................................29
  Why Videos Go Viral?..30
  Viral Marketing Examples......................................30
Social Media Marketing 32
  Facebook Marketing 32
    Ad Campaigns..33
    Facebook Pixel...33
  Twitter Marketing...34
    Twitter Lists and Chat...34
    Promoted Tweets and Ad Campaigns.................34
    Twitter Marketing Example.................................35
  Instagram Marketing 36
    Ad Campaigns and Influencers............................36
    Engagement Rate...37

  Instagram Marketing Example...........................37
 Pinterest Marketing..38
  Pinterest Boards..38
 YouTube Marketing...39
Search Engine Optimization......................................40
 On-Page SEO...40
 Off-page SEO..41
Marketing Funnels...43
 TOFU...43
 MOFU..43
 BOFU...44
Providing Value Upfront...46
 How to Provide Value...46
 Providing Value Upfront Example........................46

Forces in the Marketing Environment

As an entrepreneur, it's important to realize that your business exists within an environment that is influenced by multiple forces, and these external forces can play a defining role in the success or failure of your business. let's look at these forces.

Demographic and Cultural Understanding

As a business, you may need to constantly analyze your target demographic because this variable is critical to the success of your business. For example, a change in the generational makeup of the society will have a direct impact on businesses that target people in a certain age group or ethnicity. You may have also seen many brands that used to be around when you were younger, but they are no longer in business because they failed to accommodate new trends in their industry. An example of this trend is the department store JC Penney. The store used to be popular among shoppers, but it started losing market share to cheaper clothing brands during the recession and they also did not have a focused strategy to compete against brands like Walmart and Amazon. Besides not strategizing properly, they are also facing stiff competition from newcomers like Nordstrom, along with discount brands like Ross. JC Penny has closed many of its retail stores and are dependent upon their online and catalog business.

Microeconomic Understanding of The Economy

Besides understanding the larger picture of the economy, for effective marketing, you must find out if the consumer has the power to buy what you are offering them. The current economic conditions may have decreased the purchase power of your target audience, so you may need to rethink or repackage your products and services.

Technological Changes

These days online marketing is an essential component or the marketing strategy of most businesses. With the rise of online retail Giants like Amazon, consumers have become accustomed to buying various products online. As a marketer, you now have the ability to reach your audience without breaking your budget and refining your marketing strategy easily and efficiently with online advertising tools.

Competing with Others

Regardless of your niche, you will likely have people trying to outdo you. To compete with these businesses, you will have to not only learn the ropes but also make a marketing strategy that create some type of differentiating factor that people can easily see . For example, if you are competing with bigger brands that deal in standard and discount products, then you may have to differentiate yourself by going the premium route.

Perfecting the Sales Pitch

Coming up with the right sales pitch is a multi-step process that starts with knowing who you are selling to. The industry term used here is "positioning" and it means answering the question why someone will choose your product. In essence you must find out your distinctive competence as this competence will ensure that you can sustain your competitive advantage. A good example here is that of Apple. Apple has a number of distinctive competencies including innovation, quality of marketing, and strong performance as a brand. These competencies means that despite the higher price tag of many of their products, people consider them to be a status symbol and a reliable brand.

The 7 Ps of Marketing

To understand how to create the perfect sales pitch, let's see how Apple does the 7s of marketing: product, price, promotion, placement, people, process, and physical evidence.

Product
In terms of their products, Apple differentiates themselves by creating a luxury brand that offers stylish products and frequently introduces new innovations as well. In terms of hardware advancements, some of the big ones include iPhone 6 Plus (first large screen 5.5″ diagonal), iPhone 7 Plus (dual camera), iPhone X (OLED display), and iPhone Xs Max (6.5" OLED display). Because Apple does not allow the manufacture of its products, it is able to offer an ecosystem of products that integrate with other products and services authored by Apple.

Price
As mentioned above, in terms of price, Apple focuses on customers who are prepared to pay a premium price for a Phone, although with their recent iPhone XI announcement, they have introduced budget versions of their products as well, a sign that they are adjusting to the competition provided by Samsung , Huawei, and other brands. Also, Apple makes it easier for customers to stay within the ecosystem by offering complementary products and services .

Promotion
Product promotion is one of the strongest attributes of Apple. From Steve Jobs' famous product reveals to their "Think different" and "If you don't have an iPhone, you don't have an iPhone" campaigns, you will be hard-pressed to find a company that does marketing as well as Apple. The website Pitchskills has done a detailed analysis of Steve Jobs' sales pitches, from the opening to introducing the problem and providing the solution and benefits. Another benefit of analyzing Apple's marketing campaigns is that they have been around for a long time so you can see their marketing evolve from when they were a small company trying to compete against bigger brands two their present position as an industry leader. In 2017, CNET published a piece on Apple's ad campaigns. The article includes their campaigns from the 80s and 90s all the way up to recent campaigns.

Product Placement
With product press placement, Apple follows a hybrid distribution strategy, meaning they use their own outlets and service providers. In their own stores and service provider stores, they allow users to test drive the phones and sign the contract then and there. With the online stores, they require customers to create an Apple account to purchase the Phone.

People
The sales assistant at stores help creating brand awareness then providing people with useful information about company products and services. Steve Jobs was also known as a CEO who wasn't media shy and engaged with the people to tell his story as well as build the Apple brand. Apple also place a lot of importance on user privacy and data security. For example, the company stayed firm on their principles of user data protection in a famous data encryption case.

Process
The process that creates the innovations Apple is known for is very detail oriented. An article published by the Pragmatic Institute gives an insight into this process. In the article, author Alain Breillatt, mentions that "Apple designers expect to design 10 different mockups of any new feature under consideration. And these are not just crappy mockups; they all represent different, but good, implementations that are faithful to the product specifications."

The article also mentions Steve Jobs saying that the company does not do any market research. "We figure out what we want. And I think we're pretty good at having the right discipline to think through whether a lot of other people are going to want it, too." Of course, as an industry leader Apple has more wiggle room than a starter, but many startups are also trying to disrupt and anticipate their disruption will be accepted by the public.

Physical Evidence
Apple's packaging strategy is also one of their distinguishing features, both in terms of the box that the product comes in and the services that are packaged with the product, such as Apple care. Staying up to date with the need for environmentally friendly packaging, Apple released their paper and packaging strategy in 2017 and changed the iPhone 7 case material from petroleum-based plastic to fiber.

With all these processes working correctly for you, it becomes easier to deliver a clear sales pitch that includes problem that customers are experiencing and solutions to solve that problem. A sales strategy can include in number of steps, some essential others optional. In the following chapters I will discuss, these steps and how you can use them to improve your sales strategy.

Persuasive Storytelling

Storytelling allows you to connect with your customers at a deeper level than the consumer and seller level. Stories are effective because they connect with people at a level that simple facts can't. By making things relatable, you allow people to act based on the connection you have created with them. At its core , a story should have a message to give to the listeners. And, this message should be based on what you want others to do and why they should do it.

Also, storytelling is not limited to promoting a finished product. You can also use it to promote your idea and for motivating your team . The key point here is to find an example that fits the situation. Figure out what others are doing and how it relates to what you are doing. Besides using emotion and good examples, also include facts and to your message.

Storytelling Examples

A good example of brand storytelling by a major brand is that of Airbnb. Their idea is to encourage people to have a local travel experience. One of the ways they encourage people is by informing them about how people are using their rentals when vacationing in popular tourist spots.

Another example is that of dating app Hinge. The company markets itself as an alternative to the market leader Tinder. Commenting on their approach founder and CEO of hinge says, "We're trying to capture the people who are graduating from swiping service to look for a relationship, who know that means putting yourself out there and being more real and vulnerable."

Another story is that of Mars' Maltesers campaign. Chocolate manufacturer learned that 4/5th of disabled people feel that they are underrepresented in TV and media. Based on this information , they created a series of three humorous ads that were inspired by the stories of disabled persons.

According to Michele Oliver, VP of marketing at Mars Chocolate UK, they were looking to diversify communication and learned that they can also do better at representing the different people who buy their products.

These ads were the first step for the brand. Moving forward they wanted to ensure that, when they are planning for the main character in an ad, they look at various factors including ethnicity, disability and nature of the family, added Michelle. "The second thing that we are going to do is to look at diversity as a creative springboard to unlock creativity on some of our existing campaign ideas and how that might unlock even better and more effective advertising for us going forward. Then the third step internally is whether there are any brands, and we haven't answered this yet, that we can use diversity as a platform in a way that Lynx recently have."

Lynx, called Axe in many countries, created ad "find your magic" featuring various men. This contrasts with you usually see with axe and other competitors of the body spray. Global VP of the two brands, Rik Strubel, said "We have been catering to teenage guys and we are now talking to his older brother, who is in university."

Lead Optimization

Lead generation has changed in many ways. It used to be about finding customers now with many customers using the Internet to find companies, being found by these customers has become a key to success. Similarly, advertising to a mass audience has decreased in popularity, as we get accustomed to using tools that allow extremely detailed and narrow targeting based on consumer behavior.

Challenges with Lead Generation

Let's look at some of the challenges faced by businesses in the lead generation process . The challenges include: lack of high-quality data to drive campaigns, lack of budget , inability to create meaningful content, lack of insight into the target audience, balancing between strategic thinking and execution after plan.
Of course, some of these issues such as budget and lack of resources require more than skill to solve. But in terms of the approach you need to take to optimize your leads, consider the following options:

Nurturing Approach
To make more people engage with your message, take a nurturing approach towards them. Provide them quality information on a consistent basis and tailor that information according to your relationship with them. If they are in new subscriber, get them the time to familiarize themselves with your business before presenting them with an offer. For nurturing, you would need to figure out is your messaging style. This will be a trial and error process, so be patient and continue working until you come up with effective messages.

Data Enrichment
A concept many businesses are using today's data enrichment. With data enrichment, businesses combine the raw data about customers with publicly available data such as social media content and socioeconomic data. In this process of deep segmentation, businesses identify customer groups more precisely than if they just used demographic or behavioral data.

Sales Qualified Lead (SQL)
To identify leads, you need to define what constitutes a Sales Qualified Lead (SQL) or hot lead. For example, if you're offering a demo of your website, does the person who sign up to receive that demo can be considered a lead even when we don't know if they have actually read what's written in the freebie. Of course, businesses use the practice of sending information and offers to all the people they have in their email database, but further insight will be needed to divide that email list into is regular and high-quality leads.

Lead Optimization Examples

One example of lead generation success is that off TUI, which has over 180 brands and over 30mil customers. as mentioned above , creating quality content to engage the audiences the challenge with lead generation. They were failing to generate enough leads and nurturing their customers with their email marketing campaigns the brand decided to implement an inbound marketing strategy.

"For everything we've been doing, one of our biggest goals is to improve organic search rankings and leads. We're trying to push much content entry like blogging, landing pages and social media" said Rebecca Heidgerd, Director of E-Commerce for TUI North American Education.

By blogging once a week, using hub sports blogging tools, they were able to exponentially increase their social media traffic, web site visits. for their bright spark Canada brand, they were able to increase their year annual leads by 128%. Instagram it is a platform that lends itself well to storytelling. Beside telling the story with pictures businesses are also using it to create short stories called in soccer and stories . An example of using the tools provided by Instagram to build a business following is that of Jason stone. Jason stone Just before joining Instagram, but it was on Instagram that he was able to is each over 2,000,000 followers through his millionaire mentor Instagram feed. Instagram success translates into $100,000 per month according to him. he was able to use his online presence to start a local advertising business without the need of any traditional advertising. Called local door coupons, the business has a franchise model and enables local advertisers a low-cost option for placing their advertisements on the door steps of local customers.

Post-Sale Follow Up

Following up on the sale is something many businesses do wrong. They either overdo the product promotion or contact the customer only when they are looking to make a new sale. Instead you should take a reassuring approach, using messages like "we are here to help" and also checking in on the customer, asking if they are happy with their purchase. Here the idea is to keep the lines of communication open. Besides asking about customer experience, you can also use the information the customer has provided to personalize messages. For example, you can send them a message on the milestone they have completed with your company. Based on their customer history you can also informed them about products, books, websites and invite them to event that match their interests.

Frequency of Follow-ups

With follow-ups, the question is how many times you should contact a person before giving up? Some believe that you should contact until you get a response, regardless of how many times you must contact them or what they say in response. Of course, this approach is supported by the marketing rule of 7, according to which prospects need to hear your message 7 times before they will buy what you are selling. However, things have changed thanks to social media. the rule of 7 was first heard of in the 1930s in the movie industry. Today online marketing has made it very easy and cost effective to show your many many times if needed and target is a specific audience as well.

Post-Sale Follow-Up Examples
So, should you be using the rule of 7 with your email marketing campaigns? Let's look at what stats had to say about this. According to research published on woodpecker, the reply rate of emails was 9% when 1 to 3 emails were sent in a sequence and 27% when 4-7 emails were sent in a sequence. According to a study of cold calls and emails, 93% of converted leads were reached by the 6th call attempt. In other words , you will have most of your conversions by call number six so you can limit the number of calls you make to perspective customers to six instead of going for call number 7,8, 9 and onwards. Also, calling the prospect within a minute of receiving a lead improved conversion by 391%.

Smart Trials and Onboarding Customers

Offering something that provides value and convinces people to find out more is the main challenge with trial offers . Research shows that 40 to 60% of free trial users (software and SASS users in this case) will only use the product once. Ideally you want the customer to sign up quickly and make a decision about whether they will use the product long-term. So how can one be smart about offering trial versions?

Length of The Trial

One feature that you will decide is the length of the free trial. Some believe that having a short trial is better because it will increase the likelihood that people will use the product more during the time it's available to them for free, which in turn will make them make up their mind. The length of your free will vary depending on your product or service. For example, users may be able to make up their mind about a VPN service in a few uses, but will require more time to evaluate an email marketing program.

Trial Offer Example

Customer success solutions company to Totango analyzed the success rates of the trials offered by companies. according to them, majority of companies had a conversion rate of less than 8% but some companies we're able to convert as much as 20%. Two of the important factors with the good conversion rates were the simplicity of the sign on process and easy workflows, according to CEO of Totango Guy Nirpaz.
To understand how companies, react to unresponsive followers users, the company signed up for 10 name-brand trial services and did not use any of them. Six companies did not follow up. However, some companies did follow up with personalized offers , sent via email, offering their support. Some companies

also provided the contact information of an actual person for the help. Also, 60% companies used the customer's name. Besides communicating with the non-users, the better companies also increased their engagement as the trial progressed. One of the companies, Jive, engaged by sending a personal message from a success coach along with their contact information.

The type of trial you offer is also a function of your current goals. For example, Dropbox allows users to continue using the tool for free as long as their storage does not exceed 2 gigabytes. at the same time, they offer users to upgrade to one terabyte for a free. this freemium trial strategy has worked for the company well as it has been able to generate 1 billion in revenue in 2017 with a paid customer base of 11million, according to HBR. Drop box has been pursuing this freemium strategy for a long time. In 2012, Dropbox co-founder Drew Houston said that "If people aren't using it, they'll never pay. If lots are using it, we think they'll come." Dropbox could afford to pursue this strategy at that time as well because you're tired the funds. other businesses may not be able to sustain the freemium model. for a startup that has a limited supply of cash, the cost of offering premium version may make may not make sense. Also, there is the risk that people will see the product as a free product and continue using it but won't go for the paid version.

Onboarding Customers

Another important point when it comes to trial offers is making the trial as easy as possible for them so they can get onboard with you. On boarding is all about showing the customer the value the product can offer and getting them excited about using the product. Effective on boarding will require constant communication and helping customers create measurable goals they can achieve by using the product. When providing information, make sure you are selective about what you share with them. Tools like guided tours and set-up wizards really help with the on boarding process, because they allow you to disseminate information in a step by step manner. Another feature you can consider is too have explanation clouds or banners for the functions customers will see when they start using the product.

With customer onboarding, you will often hear the term churn rate. Churn rate means the rate of customers who stop using your product. Make it your goal to decrease the churn rate by providing value and explaining the value you are providing throughout your engagement with the customer.

Onboarding Example

A good example of on boarding customers is that off Dropbox box. When you use drop box for the first time, it asks you several questions to understand your purpose of using the tool. Based on the answers you provide, Dropbox personalize itself for you.

Time Marketing

Time marketing is all about finding the right time to release the product into the market. To understand time marketing, let's look at the prerequisites for it. The two prerequisites to time marketing are correct identification of the target market and the ability to track the targeted audience.

Questions for Time Marketers

Some of the questions that a time marketing team addresses include:
Is there a specific time of the year when the product should be launched? For some companies it's easier to answer this question than others. For example, it will be easier for a company to target Christmas than target people who use swimwear. With Christmas you can easily find the window within which you will launch the product, but with swimwear you will have to figure out whether it will make more sense to launch the product before summer or during the winter holidays when many people go to warmer climates.
Besides deciding on a suitable time, the marketing team will also have to stay abreast of the condition of the market. Is the product as popular as it was during initial research or has there been a change in popularity?
The team will also have investigated the timing of the advertising campaign in relation to the launch and if competitors are launching their products, and the scheduled release dates of those products. If you're in a market there are competitors who are equally popular or more popular than you, then releasing your product at the same time as them might mean that you get affected by the buzz around their product launch.
If your company has more than one product to offer, then you will also have to consider the product life cycle of your current

products. Many companies start developing their new product before the old product is still gaining popularity. The best time to release a new product is when the old product is peaking, because at this time you already have the customer's interest. Finally, you should also develop a plan for a field product launch.

Remember if the product launch fails, it does not mean you had the wrong idea. Sometimes the required consumer education leads to failure. For example, the 2004 launch of a scent player by P&G failed. Called Scentstories, the product had the design of a CD player and emitted every 30 minutes. For the product launch, the company hired the singer Shania Twain. This caused confusion because many people thought the device involved both scents and music. In the case of Scentstories, an educational campaign may have helped customers understand the product.

PAS System

PAS stands for problem, agitate, solution. It's a formula that many people use to create the content for their copywriting materials. The idea here is to identify the biggest problems your customers are facing, then remind them of the negative effects of that problem can have on them, and, finally, provide them with a way to solve the problem.

Problem

Start by attempting to understand the problem. Let's take a simple example: If someone is looking for a hair growth formula, they want to fix their baldness problem. Understand the reasons why they want to fix their baldness. This will be the problem your product must solve.

As you go deeper into the issue , you will come across the questions your customers will have in mind when searching for your product. You will learn more about their fears and frustrations. You will find out how the problem makes them feel. You will also learn about other products they are using and if they are satisfied or unsatisfied with those products.

Of course, with data analytics tools available today you can find more about your customers quicker including the exact search queries they're making online. Use these tools to your advantage to find a way to relate to their problems.

An important part of this step to choose a voice for your message that your audience will be able to relate to. This means thinking and talking like them.

Agitate

As the name of the step suggests, the second part of this strategy is about explaining how the problem can impact your customers if it gets worse. The idea here is to create urgency so you can encourage him to act when you provide a solution in the next step.

There are different techniques you can use to agitate. One way is to provide an example from real life. Someone who has gone through similar situation as your target audience and how the issue has affected their life.

However, while agitating, avoid going too far. Don't Make your customers focus on the story and forgot about the solution. End your story with a way out for them.

Solution

This part is all about relieving the pain. Provide the solution you have to offer and ask your audience to act.

The PAS system for copywriting forces you to think about the real problems your target audience is facing and how you can connect with them at an emotional level.

PAS Example

To discuss the use of this formula, let's consider the example published by Demian Farnworth Published on Copyblogger: "Insecure? You're not alone. Millions of people admit to being insecure. Yet, remain that way and you'll live a life in the shadows. A life on the fringe. Always wishing, never doing. Fortunately, there's an answer."

Demian Created this copy for promoting Airtel evangelists, whose work was the answer in this case. He further adds that PAS is a time saver then it comes to social media marketing and evaluate the content of other people when you're looking for something to share.

Finding Specific Referrals

Referrals are a consistent way to grow your business and research also backs the importance of referrals. According to Nielsen research, 84% of people trust recommendations from people they know, also called earned advertising, and 78% said that they trust consumer opinions that are posted online. As a business looking for referrals , you often ask your connections to refer anyone who may be interested in your service. However, this form of advertising doesn't really produce the results in most cases. They may be not interested in convincing others of your idea or they may simply don't have the time. One way you can make the process easier for them is to give them specific template to use for the referrals. A template allows you to write down what you want to convey to the potential client. With a template in hand, your connection will be able to simply forward the information they get from you.

When talking about referrals you should also remember went to not ask for a referral. You should not ask for a referral immediately after making a sale. Instead, at that moment, you should be focused on creating a sense of engagement with your new clients as quickly as possible. Go beyond the sale and try to understand why the customer is buying the product. Include a relatable story about another customer and how you have developed a good relationship with them through your customer service. Taking the time to get to know the customer may ultimately be the best way to get a referral.

Referral marketing is big on social media. Businesses offer their products for free to these influencers to it review their products in their social media content. While social media referral marketing is used for all demographics, Internet savvy millennials are one of the main targets of campaigns. In the US, 80 million millennial shoppers spent $600 bn in 2017, and are projected to spend $1.4 tr by 2020, according to referral marketing expert Extole. Here are some success stories of businesses targeting this demographic.

Referral Marketing Examples

Julep: Julep is a Seattle, WA-based beauty brand with a subscription model that allows millennials to use latest beauty products without going over their budget. In their camping with Extole, they rewarded referrers with $15 credit and a free beauty box per registered referral. Once per month, the company asked advocates to personalize their beauty box and asked them to spread the word to "get $15 for every friend who joins" via a popup display. The referral generated 5 times the shares they got on any other day of the month.

The company's marketing strategy connects the acquisition of new customers to the targeting ability of present customers. It incentivizes brand advocates to target specific people who will be interested in the company's product.

One of the biggest examples of the referral program success is that of Uber. The company used referrals to not only expand within the US but also to over 50 countries worldwide. According to the nature of their business, they run two different referral programs – one for the drivers and one for the ride users. The riders get a free ride equaling a certain amount of money for using the app for the first time. With Uber, many current users invite others to use the app. Also, if you're friend chooses your code to sign up, both of you receive referral credits , according to ReferralCandy. For the drivers, the rewards are larger. up to $500 if the driver signs up with their own cars and up to $1750 if the sign up with a rental.

Drop box is another company that used referral marketing to its advantage. Understanding the market for storage, they offered free 500MB space for both the user and the referred user, enabling them to significantly increase signups.

Viral Marketing

Like its name, viral marketing has spread like a virus among businesses looking to market online. The idea here is to create content that will spread quickly online through algorithms favoring the content and users of popular social media platforms and communities sharing the content with their followers and others. There is no restriction on the type of content that can go viral online. Depending on the platform, you can find viral videos, images and articles.

Viral Marketing Platforms

In terms of the best platforms for viral marketing, you can find all the big social media names here, including Facebook, YouTube, Reddit, Twitter, Instagram, Pinterest, etc.
Each platform is slightly different from the other. Facebook is the popular platform with Over 2.3 B monthly users. It can be described as a personal platform where people come to connect with their friends and share posts from community and business pages. YouTube has 2 B active users and it's the popular choice for following vloggers, infotainment, how-to content and age-restricted content. These two sites feature prominently in many of the video marketing campaigns you may have heard of. How effective are these two sites in making content go viral? let's look at some stats as of May 2019.

Why Videos Go Viral?

So, what are the factors that make content go viral? Explore this question, let's consider a study on what makes in nonprofessional video go viral. The study involved understanding the reason behind the video "I'm farming, and I grow it" going viral. The study concludes that "the key components for making a non-professional video go viral are "opinion leaders" spreading the message and video content that elicits positive feelings such as joy, humor, or praise." The study also provides a model for making videos go viral. The model is based on previous research in this case.
According to Business Insider, the main emotions that make things spread like crazy online include: awe, laughter, amusement and enjoy. other factors include anger, empathy , surprise , sadness and other factors. the research involved analyzing 10,000 of the most Shared articles.
As part of the research, they also interviewed 2500 people to determine why they share the content they share online and found the following reasons:
"Bring valuable and entertaining content to one another.
Define themselves to others (give people a better sense of who they are)
Grow and nourish relationships (stay connected with others)
Self-fulfillment (to feel more involved in the world)
Get the word out on causes they care about"

Viral Marketing Examples

Among the fastest viral video, the rings hidden camera prank ranks no.1 as it got 200 million views in the first 24 hours on Facebook. The second most viewed video was "Boy with Luv" by BTS (ft. Halsey) with 74.6 million views on YouTube. And, in 3rd position was "Me!" by Taylor Swift with

65.2 million views on YouTube. While many of the entries in the most fastest viral videos include prominent singers with strong marketing budgets, overall, viral marketing does need a big budget.

Another study found that "while first-degree friends are important for initial marketing, second- and third-degree friends are essential for "viral" spread."

The study also found that video ratings play their part as well, and it doesn't matter whether they are positive or negative. One of the prominent examples of this phenomena is the "Friday" song by Rebecca Black.

She released her music video on YouTube in Sep 2011. In a matter of days, the video become popular globally. The song was criticized for its lyrics and video concept. As of Oct 7, 2019, the song has 136 million views and she has 1.46 million subscribers on the platform.

Social Media Marketing

Social media marketing used to be a smaller part of businesses strategy but with the popularity of social media platforms and the development of targeted and cost-effective advertisement tools by these platforms, social media marketing has become bigger and bigger. research suggests that 90% of customers of a brand have used social media to communicate with that brand, 63% of customers expect brands to provide customer service through their social media, and 71% of customers who like the social media service they got from their brand are likely to refer others to the products and services of that company.

Businesses use social media marketing for both lead generation and increasing audience engagement. The marketing can be divided into paid advertisements and promotions and community-based marketing. So, where should a brand go to market their products? While businesses usually have it presents on multiple platforms, the right platform for that will depend on the nature of their business. Let's look at some of the important platforms businesses are using it to their advantage.

Facebook Marketing

Over 50 million small businesses use Facebook Pages to connect with their customers and four million of those businesses pay for social media advertising on Facebook. Also, 97% of B2C marketers and 89% of B2P marketers use the platform, according to Hootsuite.

Here, it's important to define what is a Facebook Page. " A Facebook page is a public profile specifically created for businesses, brands, celebrities, causes, and other organizations. Unlike personal profiles, pages do not gain "friends," but "fans" - which are people who choose to "like" a page" (TechTarget).

Ad Campaigns
With FB advertising, you run ad "campaigns". The campaign consists of ad sets and you can add multiple ads to each ad set. At the ad set level, you define who the ads will target. Facebook has multiple options when it comes to targeting an ad. Besides age, gender and location, you can also target interests of people and people who are part of specific pages. For example, if you are selling a dog bed, you can target Facebook pages that discuss dogs. You can also target multiple interests of the audience. For example, you can say show a Facebook add to somebody who likes Pit Bulls and German shepherds.

Facebook Pixel
An Important tool in Facebook advertising is the Facebook Pixel. It is basically a piece of code that Facebook provides you that you put on to your website. Facebook pixel helps you track conversions, optimize ads and retarget customers.
Here, conversion means a completed action someone has taken on your website, such as subscribing to you or making a purchase. And, optimization means that FB will automatically improve ads so you can target people that are likely to convert, such as people making an inquiry on your site.
The best feature of the Pixel is retargeting. With retargeting, you can target people that have already interacted with you. And, you can retarget people based on specific actions that they took, such as adding a product to the watchlist or cart or asking a question.

Twitter Marketing

Twitter hers 330 million active users which is considerably less than Facebook and YouTube, but when it comes to popularity with B2B and B2C marketers, it's right up there with Facebook and LinkedIn. According to Hootsuite, 75% of B2B businesses market on Twitter and 65% of B2C marketers use the platform . In comparison, the stats for LinkedIn are 80% for B2B and 44% for B2C. In terms of advertising on the platform, Twitter claimed to have a 50% increase in add engagements and a 14% decline in cost per engagement in Q3 of 2018.
Twitter is a unique platform because it gives you easy access to your customers. Also, customers can directly voice their concerns with your by replying to your tweets or sending you a private message. It's a place where people have conversations about topics in a few words without going into the unnecessary details that drag the conversation.

Twitter Lists and Chat
Like Facebook, you can use Twitter for both free and paid marketing. For free marketing you can use a Twitter List to gain insights about your target audience because the list will only show the posts made by the people you include in the list. If you want to direct interaction on the topic at a given time, you can use the Twitter chat option. For chats, businesses create a unique hashtag and share that hashtag with their audience.

Promoted Tweets and Ad Campaigns
They paid options available include but promoted tweets and ad campaigns on Twitter. With the promoted tweets option, you can get Twitter to automatically promote your tweets for a set monthly fee. However, this option is only available in the US, UK and Japan , with fees of 99 USD, 79 GBP and 9900 JPY respectively.

Each day of the month, Twitter will promote 10 of your tweets. The tweets will be shown to your selected audience and become Twitter ads showing a promoted tweet icon. At the same time, Twitter will run a promoted account campaign, which according to them, will help you reach 30,000 additional people every month.

With Twitter ads you have the flexibility of setting the budget and decide what you want to achieve head your campaign -- followers , website videos visitors , video of yours , fruit engagements, etc.

Twitter Marketing Example

An example of a company using Twitter marketing the right way is the fast food chain Wendy's. The company has gotten a ton of attention and developed its relationship with their customers by regularly engaging on Twitter, showing love to fans, apologizing for bad services, and playfully criticizing competitors for their products and services.

For example, Wendy's shut down of a twitter user "Thuggy-D" who was saying that the company freezes their beef. This was picked up by CNN's Anderson Cooper. On public demand, Wendy's went on to roast CNN as well. This exchange resulted in over a 400% rise in conversation volume mentioning the food chain in a 10-day period, over 869M impressions from 222 media placements in major outlets, over 20M visits to Wendy's page on Twitter, and over 200,000 new followers, according to VML.

Wendy's popularity with customers has led to many people creating content highlighting Wendy's' tweets. Besides engaging with customers and their competitors, the fast food chain has also used some unusual promotional tactics, including a rap battle with another fast food chain Wingstop, and its mixed tape titled "We Beefin'?". Talking to Forbes chief concept and marketing officer at Wendy's, Kurt Kane, said "They (other companies) are genuinely interested in trying to understand how we do what we do," and they have been asked about their strategies by "some of the largest companies." He further added, "We want to be likable and sassy. We don't want to be seen as sarcastic and rude. But we walk a fine line. Sometimes we get it wrong in tone."

Instagram Marketing

With 1B active monthly users, Instagram is a mobile-based platform where brands go to market to the younger segments of the audience. 71% of Instagram users are younger than 35, and 72% of US teens use Instagram. In terms of use by businesses ,over 70% of US businesses use Instagram and 75% of users take action (Hootsuite).

Ad Campaigns and Influencers

You can use Instagram for marketing in multiple ways. Like Facebook, you can create your own business page and buy advertisements. But, what many businesses do with Insta is to engage influencers – These are people who have a sizable following on the platform.

Let's look at Instagram advertisements. Instagram is owned by Facebook and advertise on Instagram, you setup the ads using Facebook's platform. You will pick an objective for the campaign, such as brand awareness, engagement , reach, etc. After you create your ad, you will select Instagram as the platform to display them from the Facebook tool. Also, like Facebook, you can set the specific budget for your Instagram as well.

Engagement Rate

Influencers can be very helpful in spreading the word about your business, but with influencers you need to make sure that they have real followers. One option you have is to check the engagement rates of influencers. You can do this with a website like Influencermarketinghub.com. This engagement rate is calculated based on comments and likes. For example, if an account has 1000 followers and only 100 of them engage with the post then the engagement rate will be 1% .

research suggests engagement rates also vary according to the number of followers someone has. For example, the average engagement rate for accounts with over 1,000,000 followers is 1.97%, which is lesser than accounts with twenty 20K to 200K followers which is 2.15% and significantly less than accounts with one 2K to 5K followers who have an engagement of 5.6% . So, when choosing an influencer, make sure you measure them based on the engagement rate that's most relevant to them. In terms of overall engagement in 2019 compared to 2018, the numbers have gone up by 22 to 25%.

Instagram Marketing Example
One of the examples of successful Instagram marketing is what Adidas did with their Neo brand. They asked their users to create content that's inspired by Adidas and post it on Instagram with the hashtag #MyNeoShoot. From the people who replied, they choose the best and asked them to do photo shoot which Adidas would post on their Instagram channel. To capture the imagination of Instagram users they also used the services of the singer Selena Gomez, who has a large following on the platform. The campaign resulted in 71,000 mentions of the hashtag and 41k followers.

Another example is of the mobile game Bejeweled. The Bejeweled team enlisted top Instagram influencers, including Koya Webb, and made two YouTube shorts, featuring the popular dog JiffPom. In one month, the game Bejeweled went from 702 to 182 in the top-earning apps on Apple's App Store in the US.

Pinterest Marketing

Pinterest has 265 million monthly active users, many in the affluent middle-class category. Also, 85% of women users use Pinterest to plan "life moments," ranging from decorating a new home to party planning, and 55% of users are looking specifically for products, which is over 4x than other platforms (Hootsuite).
Like Instagram, it relies on Images to attract users. However, it's different from Instagram because Instagram is about commenting and liking pictures, while Pinterest allows you to comment on pictures, but it does not place a lot of importance on how many comments the picture has when it comes to ranking it. In fact, there are also limits on how many times you can comment per day. With less focus on the 'social' aspect of social media, Pinterest allows you to focus more on the content.

Pinterest Boards
The Pinterest setup allows you to find people interested in what you offer without a lot of followers. One of the main marketing tools in Pinterest are group boards. If you are just starting out and do not have a lot of followers, you can join group boards that other people have and you pin your own content to these people's boards, enabling their followers to notice what you are doing and become your follower. Pinterest also has an ad platform, but it's not as developed as some of the others. Also, as mentioned above, many Pinterest users are affluent, so there is a better opportunity to get a return on the time and effort you put into your marketing.

YouTube Marketing

YouTube is the premiere video marketing platform. Marketing on YouTube starts with a YouTube for business account. YouTube The account gives you access to insights into your audience's behavior, including where your videos are being viewed, what is the age range and gender of your viewers and the watch time of your content. You can also get a qualitative measure of your content by enabling comments on the videos. To engage more viewers, you can add call to actions and 6-second bumper ads to your videos. The type of ads available with YouTube include skippable video ads, non-skippable video ads, overlay ads , display ads , bumper ads and sponsored guards. If you're not interested in running a YouTube channel, you can use these ads to promote your business on the 2nd most popular social media platform. YouTube community is also filled with influencers like Instagram, so you can partner with an influencer to get more out of your campaigns.

With social media networks, you can also find many communities that are specific to certain topic such as [Warrior Forum](#) is for internet marketing professionals and freelancers offering their services online and [RoadSTR](#) is in network for car enthusiasts.

Search Engine Optimization

Search engine optimization (SEO) is the strategy businesses use to rank themselves in this search engines organically. The benefit of search engine is that it allows your web pages to get traffic without spending money on placing ads or contacting influencers to market your products. Search engine optimization is a multi-step process that includes optimizing your web pages and posting your content on social media to promote sharing and viewing of your content.

On-Page SEO

Broadly speaking, on-page SEO means improving the technical aspects of your page along with user related parameters. Here the technical parameters include site speed , H1 and H2 tags , URL, etc., and the user-related parameters include, internal and external links , fonts , images , bounce rate , click through rate (CTR), time spent on site, etc. To optimize pages for the search engine, businesses make use of keywords. Keywords are the words that users enter into search engines to find the products they're looking for. There are various tools that record these entries including Google AdSense.
On-page can also be viewed in terms of providing value to the user and satisfying the search engine algorithms that rank websites. The content you post on your page needs to satisfy both your readers and the boards . For this purpose, there are certain practices such as including your keyword in the title of your article, using subheadings to help search engines understand your content better , linking to other pages on the website , providing title and tag for the images you use. For example, if you're writing a blog post about gardening tools , you will search for keywords that people use to find those tools and include your main keyboard in the title of the article. If you choose to use some images along with the text, you will

add your keyword phrase in the name of the image and alt tag. Similarly, you will optimize your meta description , which is the description for the search engines, by using the keyboard there as well. Besides this content , businesses also look to optimize the address of their website by including relevant keywords in the name of the website.

Off-page SEO

Off-page SEO is about building links with quality websites and creating a following for the business on social media . The link building exercise you will do should focus on websites that have a good reputation and ranking . Here ranking means the domain authority of the website and the links from a website with high authority add more valuable than links from a website with no authority.

Domain authority is a ranking score system developed by a software company Moz. The score ranges from 1 to 100 and it predicts how the website will do in the search engine rankings, also known as SERPs. According to Moz "Generally speaking, sites with a very large number of high-quality external links (such as Wikipedia or Google.com) are at the top end of the Domain Authority scale, whereas small businesses and websites with fewer inbound links may have a much lower DA score. Brand-new websites will always start with a Domain Authority score of one." Domain authorities also is fluctuating thing, so you must be actively involved in maintaining your domain authority .

With paid marketing you are guaranteed that your target audience will see your message , but with search engine optimization you don't have the same guarantee. However, if done right, SEO will allow you to reach the top pages of search engines and get a return on your investment with the visitors you find.

In terms of targeting a search engine for SEO, Google is still the best option. The search engine makes up about 79% of global desktop search traffic, followed by Bing at 7.27%, Chinese search engine Baidu at 6.55% and Yahoo at 5.06%, according to Impactbnd.

Marketing Funnels

A marketing funnel, or sales funnel, shows your customer's journey with you, from when they learn about your business to conversion. It allows you to visualize the customer's journey in the form of steps involved in it. The funnel has evolved from the "AIDA" model created by Elias St. Elmo Lewis. This model shows that a sale involves the following four elements: Awareness (The prospect knows about the problems and their possible solutions), Interest (The prospect is interested in the product), Desire (The prospect evaluates the brand), and Action (The prospect buys or does not buy the product).
The marketing funnel has three distinct elements collectively called "TOFU-MOFU-BOFU," and the three refer to top, middle, and bottom of the funnel respectively.

TOFU

At the first stage of the funnel, you have prospects who are aware of their problems and are looking for solutions. They become interested in articles , videos , products that provide solutions and are open to more information on the subject.

MOFU

At this stage, the customers are evaluating the different brands they know about by listening to people advocating for these grants and the opinion of customers who are satisfied with the products
As a business, you know about the needs and wants of your customers and you can position yourself as a solution provider they can depend on. Of course , many people are hesitant to buy before testing or sampling the product. For example, if you're selling a car, you will offer them to test drive it before

discussing further. Similarly, if you're offering an antivirus software, you will provide them a trial version that will expire after a few days. The idea is to convince them to make a micro transaction that is designed to help them understand what's on offer and help you make the sale afterwards.

BOFU

At this stage, the buyer knows the problem they are facing, the options that can potentially help them solve the problem, so they are able to make a decision. At this stage you can help them make up their mind by sharing success stories of others who have used the product . By now, you have done your job in convincing them to use your product. Now, it's up to them to buy the product or not.

Some businesses consider this a complete marketing funnel , but many businesses have added two more stages to these stages: loyalty and advocacy. If you are successful in making a sale, it's time to build a long relationship with the customer. This long relationship starts by reassuring them of their decision and continue with offering them a discount and keeping them in the loop about your products and services on a regular basis. It also involves encouraging them to advocate for your services. Some company incentivize this advocacy by offering rewards to the advocates and also to the people they bring in.

When talking about funnels, it's is also important to know some terminology related to them. Marketers often refer to the leads they find as cold, warm and hot or qualified.

Cold Lead: A prospect who fits your client profile but hasn't shown interest in your product.

Warm Lead: A person who has shown some form of interest in your business.

Hot Lead: A customer has indicated that want to discuss purchasing your product.

Providing Value Upfront

An experienced business person will know that they will get a certain value by using your product or service. For them you will have to go the extra mile to earn their business.

How to Provide Value

This involves providing great up-front value that's may not directly related to the deal but directly related to the person who you are selling to. The value you provide can be anything that enhances their reputation or the reputation of their business. Think of this upfront value as the gift you provide to anyone who is interested in your service.

Providing Value Upfront Example

Another strategy many companies use is to provide a valuable product that compliments other products they offer. For example, foam case company MyCaseBuilder.com allows users to use its custom foam case software for free. The customers use the software tool make designs that the company offers to build for them.
similarly, with many web-based businesses offer 3 reports that contain helpful information but are also designed to encourage readers to find more about that topic by becoming it appeared member.

Disclaimer

The sole purpose of this book is to provide information. The information contained in this book is provided on an as is basis, and the author is not responsible for the accuracy of information provided in the book.

The content within this book has been derived from various sources. The reader should consult professionals before implementing any advice mentioned in the book. Under no circumstances will any blame or legal responsibility be held against the publisher, or author, for any damages, reparation, or monetary loss due to the information contained within this book.

Copyright © 2019 Felix Kaufman
All Rights Reserved.

ISBN: 9781703632965

www.ingramcontent.com/pod-product-compliance
Lightning Source LLC
Chambersburg PA
CBHW031501210526
45463CB00003B/1027